The Journey to Success

Entrepreneurship 101 for Aspiring Women

Angela K. Chambers

Disclaimer

The Journey to Success: Entrepreneurship 101 for Aspiring Women

Angela K. Chambers

any person or entity with respect to any loss or damage caused or alleged to be caused directly or indirectly by this book.

This book is published by P&J Publishing Inc. The publishing company can be contacted through their official website, http://pandjpublishing.com/, or email address, info@pandjpublishing.com.

The address of publishers is as follows:

2629 E 36th St N
Tulsa, OK 74110

About the Author

Angela K. Chambers is a Business Coach, Author, Publisher, and Serial Entrepreneur. She recently launched P&J Publishing, Inc. and is a contributing blogger for P&J Publishing and 918 Lady Business Blogger. Her desire is helping others to take their passion from hobby to empire through realistic and practical actions of success.

Angela holds a Master's degree in Entrepreneurial Studies from Langston University. From the same university, she also earned a Bachelor of Arts in Business Administration and received Entrepreneurship training from the Ready Set Go Foundation.

One of Angela's biggest roles, however, is in her company LasTop Lawn Maintenance & Landscaping, Inc. Angela has been able to use her education and industry experience to gross millions of dollars in revenue for the company. She is also the founder of LasTop Lawn Care Empire Program.

In this coaching program, entrepreneurs learn the strategies and techniques needed to start and grow long-lasting lawn care businesses. Having seen many companies fail during her career, it is her mission to guide others in finding just as much success as she and her companies have.

Outside of this and her numerous other roles, Angela enjoys studying the Bible, reading, writing, learning and traveling. More than anything, and above it all, she loves spending her free time with her husband, children, and grandchildren.

Dedication
Just Live by the Faith

Then the Lord answered me and said:

"Write the vision;
Make it plain on tablets,
So he may run who reads it."

-    **Habakkuk 2:2**

I am so thankful to be chosen for a time such as this! This book is dedicated to EVERY woman desiring to change the trajectory of not only their lives but the ones they love. Not only can you positively impact everyone around you, but also change society for better.

Have faith that your Father in heaven has an even greater plan. He will far exceed that which is written for His glory!

Acknowledgments

This journey just would not be the same without my husband, Robert "Tim" Chambers, Sr., in my life. I am thankful for the chance of life with you! I know that you have my back and will always pick up the slack. You inspire me, daily. I am so blessed.

I love you!

My girls, with every task and goal I set and every journey I take, I pray that you will always be inspired to do better, live better, and be better than who you were the day before. I love each of you always and forever!

My Grandma Tee aka Wilma Factory Phifer Green: It's because of you that I have so much goodness in me. I love you, love you, love you!

To all my grandchildren: I love you, my mini kidpreneurs!

Cyndi McGhee, CPA, and owner of NextGen Tax Services, GIRL! Thank you for following your dreams and making it possible for entrepreneurs to get a sky view of all the good they can do with their business. YOU ROCK!

I am so thankful for my forever friends; Darla Viney, LaKesa Mace and Tonya Bowie. I love you, ladies, always and I'm very fortunate to have you in my life.

My big cousins Joe Phifer, Jr. and Triena Phifer have always supported my good efforts. I celebrate them!

Thank you for your unconditional love and for being great role models.

And lastly, I would like to mention Saniya Khan who encouraged me and kept me on track with my goals. She is an experienced Content Writer who is also a contributor to the book and helps me with blog writing. Thanks for pushing me!

If you are ready to see what your empire looks like get your glasses, paper, and pen. LET'S GO!

Table of Contents

1. Introduction

Your future lies in your hands. You can step into your own destiny and GO while creating a positive change in society. In fact, you can play a positive role in improving the economic situation of your country.

Wondering how to achieve the aforementioned goals? The answer is simple. Get ready to enter the world of entrepreneurship!

Back in the day, it wasn't easy for women to comfortably work in professional environments, let alone launch their own business. Fortunately, the modern era has brought a positive change in the mindset of society.

Today, 36% of businesses in the US are owned by females that create 15% of employment opportunities for the talented workforce.

Don't these statistics excite you and give the boost to plan your business venture? This is just the introduction of the book. By the time you finish reading this book, I'm sure you will be on your way to make your dreams come true.

It's a well-known fact that more women tend to struggle with financial issues than males. In fact, 70% of the people in the US living below the poverty line are females.

These numbers are enough to make a person wonder how women can improve their financial situation and become financially independent.

While it's possible to earn a good income through a respectable job, it can't give you a sense of satisfaction and achievement associated with owning a business. Moreover, how would you cover day-to-day expenses if you suddenly lose your job?

The only way to attain job security and increase income without comprising on your personal life is to plan your entrepreneurial venture.

Successful businesspeople are never afraid to approach others to seek guidance. Not only should you learn from your own mistakes, but also learn from the experiences of others. Once you analyze the costly mistake that caused them huge losses, it will be easier for you to steer clear of them.

Another takeaway I would like to share with you is that you should refrain from comparing your failure or success with business giants. You don't know about the struggles they underwent to reach the heights where they are today.

All you need to do is to set personal and professional goals and put in your energy and efforts to achieve those objectives. Treat failures as learning steps and it won't take long before your business becomes a huge success.

Who hasn't heard about Colonel Sanders, the founder of KFC fast-food chain? Thousands of restaurants rejected his recipes. Instead of losing hope and comparing himself with others, he decided to launch his own restaurant.

If he got discouraged and dumped his business idea, no one would know his name today!

Before we proceed, I would like to share with you a quote that kept me going during tough times:

"You may be the only person left who believes in you, but it's enough. It takes just one star to pierce a universe of darkness. Never give up."

- **Richelle E. Goodrich**

Believe in yourself!

There will be times when you won't have the energy to get out of bed. However, if you believe in your dreams, nothing can stop you from emerging victorious.

The purpose of this book is to raise awareness and empower women to begin their entrepreneurial journey. Aside from highlighting different aspects of entrepreneurship, I have added achievements of female role models. You will also get to know about my own entrepreneurial journey through the book.

So, read this book to learn everything you need to know before launching a business and build a legacy through determination and hard work.

2. Entrepreneurship

Entrepreneurs are building blocks of an economy that dare to enter the world of unknown. Instead of sulking over their life, they leave their 9-to-5 jobs to take control of their destiny and launch their new business.

Many people believe that only a few selected people in this world can become successful entrepreneurs. But let me tell you that anyone can become an entrepreneur as long as they are ready to work on their innovative ideas regardless of the hardships they face during the journey.

Have you heard about HydroChem? This company is a global environmental solution provider that operates in many countries. Its founder, *Olivia Lum*, sold her house and car to launch this startup and today, she is worth more than £400 million.

Astonishing, right?

If you look around, you will find many such rags to riches examples that made their name as a successful businessperson through their persistence and efforts.

Before I share with you the success stories of some inspiring entrepreneurs, let's dig into the history of entrepreneurship.

2.1   What Is Entrepreneurship?

The term entrepreneurship isn't as new as it seems. People entered the world of business nearly 20,000 years ago when they began selling goods in exchange for food or other routine items. Entrepreneurship evolved over the centuries.

The word originates from a French word, "entreprendre", which means to initiate. It is believed that this term was first used by Richard Cantillon, an Irish economist, in 1730. Later, John Stuart Mill and Jean-Baptiste Say also mentioned the word in their writings.

Entrepreneurship refers to the process of initiating a new business on the basis of a unique idea with limited resources. While startups involve a high degree of risk, the vast scope of growth is worth taking the risk.

2.2   Entrepreneurship: Classifications

Entrepreneurial ventures can be divided into many categories. Here are a few most common types of entrepreneurship you should know:

2.2.1   Individual Startup

This type of entrepreneurship works best for individuals with dreams. Around 27 million of the US work force will leave their full-time jobs and you can become one of them by launching a new business on your own.

2.2.2   Large Business Startup

Starting large entrepreneurship requires a huge investment. Since business operations are complex, you would need to hire a big team and sufficient financial resources to support business activities.

Large-scale entrepreneurship works best in industries such as cement, engineering equipment, steel, and chemicals.

2.2.3   Non-Profit Startup

Non-profit startups are a type of social entrepreneurship. Unlike other businesses, the major purpose of this business entity is to do something good for society and make this world a better place for everyone.

Aside from arranging resources, you need to understand non-profit laws and establish a board of directors before launching your idea.

2.2.4   Joint Entrepreneurship

Joint entrepreneurship is a strategic alliance through which startups survive and grow in the competitive market. Startups, individuals or government form this partnership to capture new markets, increase profits, and stay ahead of the competition.

2.3   Myths and Misconceptions – Debunked

The idea of entrepreneurship has gained popularity during the past decade. However, many people still hesitate to work on their business ideas due to prevalent misconceptions.

Let's counter those myths with facts:

2.3.1 Not Everyone Is Cut Out for Entrepreneurship

It's a widespread myth that entrepreneurship is for those who have innate business sense along with years of experience. But don't let these negative talks stop you from working towards your dreams. You will learn everything along the way!

2.3.2 You Can't Launch a Startup without Huge Investment

Many people believe they need huge funds to support business activities. The lack of financial resources, therefore, stops them from launching a startup. But it's important to note that all your small businesses needs is your time.

Furthermore, when you engage investors, you will focus more on their interests and end up forgetting value addition to your customers. So, it's best to start small and put in your efforts to make your business a success.

2.3.3 A College Degree Is Crucial

While obtaining a business degree can help you understand business concepts, it can't outweigh the experience. So, even if you don't have an MBA degree, you can still become a successful entrepreneur.

2.3.4 Feedbacks Are Irrelevant

Not many people are capable of accepting feedback. However, constructive criticism can actually help you learn and grow. So, listen to your customers as well as investors and make the most of this advice to further improve your business idea.

2.3.5   You Can't Become a Part-Time Entrepreneur

The financial uncertainty involved with startups stops many passionate people from starting a business. To avoid this problem, you can keep your day job during the initial years and leave the job for full-time entrepreneurship once you are financially stable.

2.3.6   Targeting Broad Market Is the Way to Go

Targeting broad market doesn't always work in the favor of startups, particularly when the competition is too strong. You should rather initially target a niche market and then expand the scope of your business down the road.

2.3.7   You Don't Need Social Media Marketing

Don't shy away from promoting your startup across social media channels. Through organic and paid promotions, you can understand your target market, build a reputation, expand the customer base, and increase engagement in a cost-effective way.

2.3.8   An Idea Alone Can Change the World

Although an effective idea lays the foundation of a startup, it is not enough. Unless you develop a strategy and take action, your startup is likely to fail within a few years of its launch.

2.3.9   Startups Gain Success Overnight

Startups don't become successful overnight. The truth is that the initial three years are extremely difficult. However, if you stay focused and determined, then nothing can stop you from achieving your goals.

2.3.10 Startup Life Is Attractive

Don't you get inspired by billionaire entrepreneurs such as Mark Zuckerberg, Oprah Winfrey, and Ariana Huffington?

While entrepreneurs can attain wealth and fame down the line, it's not always easy. During the initial years, you may struggle a lot. However, you ought to hold your nerves and work hard to earn success.

2.4   Entrepreneurship in the Modern Era

The era of globalization and technology has evolved the world of entrepreneurship. Not only are people more aware of the benefits of startups, but it also encourages entrepreneurs to give back to society.

The internet gives the opportunity to connect and communicate with people in the other corner of the world. Startups are no more confined by geographical boundaries. They can offer their products and services around the globe without hassles.

Digital platforms further make it easier for businesses to conduct market research and promote their offerings without breaking the bank.

Unlike traditional marketing methods, you need not spend a huge sum on advertising when it comes to online platforms. As a result, small-scale startups with limited financial resources can compete with business giants and sustain in the long run.

2.4.1 Crowdfunding

With the advent of technology, the concept of crowdfunding came into being. Instead of relying on a small group of investors, entrepreneurs can now convince a myriad of people to invest in their venture.

For this purpose, you need to connect with potential investors through social platforms and crowdfunding websites and pitch your business ideas. If you convince them that your idea has potential, they will invest capital in your entrepreneurship.

Crowdfunding makes it easier to raise huge capital. You can learn from the experiences of established businesspeople and ask for their feedback regarding your business idea. However, before you execute a campaign, make sure your business idea is copyright protected.

Let's take a look at some of the most popular crowdfunding websites for entrepreneurs:

i.   Kickstarter
ii.   Grow Venture Community
iii. Crowdfunder
iv.   GoGetFunding

Angela K. Chambers

v. CircleUp
vi. GoFundMe

3. Women and Entrepreneurship

Entrepreneurship is the ultimate dream of every person with the goal to change this world for better. Women lead around 11.6 million businesses, making it 40% of all businesses in the US.

If we take a look at statistics from 1972, only 402,000 businesses were handled by females. In around 46 years, the numbers have increased by around 2,786%. With more and more women entering the world of entrepreneurship, this ratio is expected to significantly increase during the next few years.

Tired of the gender pay gap, social inequality, and financial struggles, women turn to entrepreneurship to control their own lives. It provides them with the opportunity to become independent, earn a good income, and become an active member of society.

3.1 Why Women Should Enter the World of Entrepreneurship

Who said women can't run an entire business organization? The truth is that females can make a business profitable in limited due to their innate skills and abilities.

3.1.1 Do What You Love

When you work as a full-time or part-time employee in a company, you are bound to perform assigned tasks. This is the reason why 52.3% of Americans are dissatisfied with their jobs.

You can rather launch your innovative business and do what you love the most. This will give you the chance to work towards your goals and stay productive and happy.

What more do you want?

3.1.2 Take Control of Your Future

With the increasing unemployment rate, job security has become a major concern around the globe. You may worry about losing your job and fail to focus on your work.

On the other hand, you can improve your financial circumstances with the help of a startup. While running a business is risky, it involves higher ROI as compared to a job.

3.1.3 Maintain Work-Life Balance

When you work as an employee, you may find it difficult to give time to your family, owing to long working hours. However, if you start a business, it may be easier for you to balance personal and professional life. This way, you can also give time to your loved ones and indulge in your favorite hobbies.

3.1.4 Become Your Own Boss

Not many people appreciate taking instructions from others. If you are a creative person, you would appreciate working on your own terms.

By entering the world of entrepreneurship, you can avoid working under a bad boss in a toxic environment. Since it's your business, you can learn a lot and work as you like.

3.1.5   Avoid the Glass Ceiling Effect

Due to the corporate glass ceiling, it's not easy for women to advance in their career and climb the ladder to reach top management positions in a company. Running your own business means you don't have to experience this barrier.

3.1.6   Empower Other Women

Through entrepreneurship, not only can you make your own dreams come true, but also help other women in your community to learn and grow.

You can create employment opportunities for others and train them to become successful professionals.

3.1.7   Self-Actualization

Self-Actualization is the major motive behind starting a new business. You get to explore your talents and achieve ultimate satisfaction. This boosts your self-esteem and motivates you to work harder.

3.1.8   Bring a Positive Change

By becoming an entrepreneur, you can bring a positive change in society. You can become an inspiration for people with dreams and work towards the betterment of society.

3.2 Challenges Facing Women Entrepreneurs

Despite the increasing number of women-owned businesses, females still encounter several issues during their journey. Here are some of these:

3.2.1 Male-Dominant Environment

Gender inequality is a truth that no one can deny. It has been long believed that only men can successfully run a business. This is why female entrepreneurs may find it difficult to be taken seriously in the corporate environment.

The problem becomes huge particularly when women start a business in a male-dominant field such as engineering, construction, and technology.

3.2.2 Limited Financial Resources

It's another challenge for business women to convince potential investors to invest in their startups. Therefore, only 25% of female entrepreneurs get outside funding for their business.

While this is a major drawback, the good thing is that women can run businesses without the intervention of investors and focus on the well-being of their target audience.

3.2.3 Hiring the Right Team

You can make your business successful if you have an efficient and sincere team to support you. In the competitive market, it's a big challenge to find the top talent, onboard them, and engage them so they stay with you for an extended period.

3.2.4 The Fear of Unknown

Entrepreneurship is a risky business. Many women bury their dreams because they are afraid they may end up losing their hard-earned money to failure.

In order to achieve success in the business world, you should be mentally strong and conquer your fear.

3.2.5 Access to Knowledge

Women don't always get access to business knowledge, tech resources, venture capital, and support systems that are crucial to effectively run a business.

The solution to this issue is that women in business should help other struggling entrepreneurs and support them in establishing their small business.

3.2.6 Cultural Boundaries

In many communities, women are discouraged to take up a job or start a business. Bound by the cultural barriers, women find it difficult to become an entrepreneur and more often than not give up on their dreams.

4. Successful Women Entrepreneurs

Back in the day, it was a prevalent misconception that women are not capable of successfully running a business. Aside from this mindset, financial constraints and pressure of society stopped many women from becoming an entrepreneur.

Fortunately, things are much better in today's world, thanks to the increasing awareness about the importance of women-led businesses.

You must have heard about the most impactful personalities from the modern era. But if you take a look at history, you will get to learn about the inspiring females that changed the world forever.

For instance, Margaret Hardenbroeck went on to become the richest woman in New York. Or Elizabeth Hobbs Keckley, who lived 30 years of her life as a slave but later became a popular fashion designer.

Such examples indicate that anyone can achieve success through their will and efforts.

4.1   Female Entrepreneurs that Are Changing the Course of the World

Now, let's read about some of the most inspiring female entrepreneurs from the 21st century.

4.1.1   Janice Bryant Howroyd

Janice Bryant Howroyd is an amazing businesswoman who proved that it's not necessary to have huge funds to launch a startup. She is the founder of ActOne Group worth more than $520 million. But it would be a surprising fact for you that she started it with an investment of only $2,400.

What made her the first African American woman to establish a billion-dollar business was her eagerness to grow. Her experience working with the Billboard magazine gave her the much-needed exposure to the business world and taught her about its ups and downs.

ActOne Group offers top-notch recruitment services and caters to the needs of global clientele. Founded in 1978, the company continues to prosper under great leadership. Despite facing racial discrimination at different stages of her life, Howroyd never let criticism stop her from achieving what she deserved.

4.1.2   Jenny Eu

Ever tried healthy and delicious nut milk by the Three Trees brand? Then your entrepreneurial mind must have wondered why the person behind this startup came up with this idea.

Jenny Eu is a San Francisco based business person who decided to launch the recipe of her grandmother as a business to enter the untapped market.

Knowing that the awareness about healthy foods is increasing, she came up with the business idea to set up a profitable business while proposing a solution to societal needs.

Jenny Eu launched Three Trees in 2013 and it didn't take long for the startup to attract a big client base, thanks to the unique beverage business idea.

4.1.3   Natasha Case

Natasha Case co-founded Coolhaus in 2009 with her now life partner, Freya Estreller. The premium ice cream is prepared from organic, hormone-free, and fair-trade ingredients.

The journey started when Natasha learned about the concept of Farchitecture or Food-Architecture. Due to the attractive idea and a wide range of tasty flavors, the ice cream brand received plenty of media coverage and got people talking in no time.

There is no doubt that the journey of this entrepreneur wasn't easy, particularly because she had to work extremely hard to make her place in the crowded market. However, she made her dreams come true through extreme efforts.

4.1.4   Daniela Corrente

Known as the founder of Reel, Daniela Corrente disrupted the e-commerce industry through her mind-blowing startup idea. She offered a solution that helps people save up for shopping so they can buy the products they want without feeling guilty.

The decision of leaving her job as Associate Creative Director at Saatchi & Saatchi was difficult, but she knew that it's worth launching your own business instead of working a 9-to-5 job all your life.

She is an inspiration for those females who have some great business ideas in mind but are afraid to leave their jobs. Corrente teaches us that if you believe in yourself and are ready to take a leap of faith, then nothing can stop you from becoming successful in life.

4.2 Lessons You Can Learn from Inspiring Female Entrepreneurs

You can learn a great deal about becoming a better person and running your business effectively from the lives of the aforementioned entrepreneurs.

We have compiled a brief list of valuable lessons for you.

4.2.1 Startup and Failure Go Hand in Hand

You will experience hardships throughout the entrepreneurial journey. Your ideas will fail time and again and you may find it difficult to run your business anymore. But failure is a part of entrepreneurship and you can't always avoid it.

So, never get disheartened from failure. Instead, you should learn from your mistakes and avoid repeating them.

4.2.2 Believe in Yourself

You will find people around you who would try to discourage you from launching your entrepreneurial venture. Keep in mind that such negativity won't affect you if you believe in yourself and want to achieve success with your hard work.

4.2.3 Your Health Is Important

When you launch a small business, you are responsible to monitor its operations and perform a myriad of tasks on your own. This can take a toll on your health.

There is no doubt that work is important, but it's crucial to set your priorities. Do not work too hard that your health deteriorates. Otherwise, it will harm you in the long run.

4.2.4 Your Instincts Will Guide You

Entrepreneurs are natural risk-takers who predict the future. If your gut feeling guides you in a certain direction, it's a good idea to follow your internal wisdom. Taking calculated risks will help you establish a sustainable business.

4.2.5 Don't Ignore Personal Life

When running a business, don't get too involved that you don't have time anymore for your family or hobbies you enjoy the most. If you balance your personal and work life, you will stay fresh and find it easier to focus on your business.

4.2.6 Don't Wait for Too Long

When it comes to a startup, timing is everything. If you have an innovative idea in mind, don't wait too long to act upon that or else your competitors will take a lead and capture market share.

4.2.7   Reach Out to Your Network

The stress of entrepreneurial life can ruin your mental health. A support network can't only help you stay positive, but they can also guide you about how to make your business a success.

You should stay in touch with your support network. Aside from seeking help, always be ready to give back to society and help aspiring female entrepreneurs by sharing your experiences. This way, you can set an example for others.

4.2.8   Never Give Up

The entrepreneurial journey is never easy and is full of bumps, twists, and turns. However, only those entrepreneurs become successful who are determined and understand ground realities.

If you keep on putting in your best efforts and stay positive, then nothing and no one can stop you from reaching your destination.

4.3   Traits of Successful Female Entrepreneurs

In the modern era, women have begun to realize the benefits of running a business. This is why they give up their job and take their future in their own hands. As a result, they can take control of the startup and avoid becoming a victim of injustice.

It's a proven fact that women tend to become better entrepreneurs than males. Let's take a look at characteristics of female entrepreneurs that helped them achieve success:

4.3.1 Passion

Female entrepreneurs climb the ladder of success because they are passionate about their business idea. They are willing to learn from their mistakes and therefore, achieve success against all odds.

4.3.2 Mental Strength

If you read the biographies of female entrepreneurs, you will learn that their mental strength helped them at every stage. If not for their determination, they would have failed long ago.

It's important to control your emotions and manage stress. Regardless of the circumstances, you should believe in you and stay focused on your goals.

4.3.3 Positive Thinking

Running a startup isn't a piece of cake. Entrepreneurial life is filled with failures. If you let negative thoughts take over your mind, you will lose hope and may end up losing your business.

Successful entrepreneurs tend to stay positive most of the time and strive to achieve their objectives. If you find it difficult to keep your thoughts under control, your support network can uplift you and help you grow.

4.3.4   Hunger for Learning

Every successful entrepreneur shares a similar mindset: They are always ready to learn and consider themselves a student throughout their lives. They learn from everyone and anyone, irrespective of their age and social status.

The business world gives you exposure to innovations around you. If you are open to new experiences, you can learn about new things every day that will benefit you in the long run.

4.3.5   Consistency

Consistency is the key to establishing a great business. Women are resilient and hardworking. They don't want to give up when it comes to developing their business. This personality trait is extremely valuable.

For instance, Ruth Fertel suffered huge losses when she first invested in a restaurant but later launched the successful venture, *Ruth's Chris Steak House*. Or Oprah Winfrey faced poverty and sexual assault at a young age but went on to become the richest African American of the 20th century.

You can learn from such entrepreneurs to overcome failure!

4.3.6   Integrity

Be it your personal or professional life, never forget your moral values. You need not indulge in immoral activities or lie to your customers to boost business profits.

When you run a business, be honest to your customers and employees. If your business dealings are transparent, people will trust you and prefer your brand over your competitors.

4.3.7 Flexibility

Flexibility is crucial for success, since it keeps your mind open and enables you to come up with a creative and effective solution for all your problems.

For instance, if a business idea fails, you can tweak it to get the desired results instead of closing the business you love.

"The measure of intelligence is the ability to change."

- **Albert Einstein**

5. Why You Should Begin Your Entrepreneurial Journey

It's estimated that 400 million people worldwide own a business, making it just 5% of the entire global population. The rest of the population avoids entering this world due to a lack of interest, fear of failure, insufficient financial resources, inadequate business knowledge, and other similar reasons.

If you're not mentally prepared, you will find a plethora of excuses to avoid launching your startup. But once you make your mind, then nothing can stop you. If you identify a problem around you and come up with a solution to resolve it, then congratulations! You are ready to become an entrepreneur.

The entrepreneurial journey consists of multiple steps that can vary depending on your approach and business model.

- ✓ **Practice Daily Routine** – It's crucial for entrepreneurs to respect time and refrain from wasting it. This habit ensures you can complete chores in a timely manner
- ✓ **Evaluate Business Idea** – Your business idea is still in the initial stage. The next step is to evaluate and polish it
- ✓ **Consult Your Mentor** – A mentor can guide you in the right direction. You should find a mentor and stay in touch with them to learn from their vast experience
- ✓ **Research** – Thorough market research is important to determine whether or not your business idea has the potential to grab the attention of the target audience
- ✓ **Set SMART Goals** – Set specific, measurable, relevant, attainable, and timely goals for your business
- ✓ **Network** – Network with like-minded people to spread awareness about your venture. You can

meet people in your community as well as contact them via social media

The beginning of the entrepreneurial journey brings along strong emotions. You would feel excited about launching a startup. But at the same time, you may feel afraid and have second thoughts.

Let me assure you that there is nothing wrong with feeling afraid as long as it doesn't stop you from reaching your dreams. So, learn to accept your fear and try to overcome it.

Now that you know how to kick start your journey, let's dig into the reasons why you should consider becoming a businessperson in the first place:

5.1 Live Your Dreams

Entrepreneurial life is quite tough, but people find it attractive because it frees them from clutches of the corporate culture. They are no longer bound by a job they despise and can workday and night to turn their dreams into reality.

When it comes to a business, it's appreciated to dream big. Although dreaming alone can't take you anywhere, you can live your dreams by working in the right direction. So, it's rightly said that you can't make it big unless you dream big.

Experienced business coaches and mentors can assist you in this regard. They can guide you about goal setting and meeting those objectives. Furthermore, they will help you avoid making costly mistakes that can ruin your business.

5.2 Achieve Sense of Satisfaction

Entrepreneurship boosts your self-esteem and provides an adrenaline rush that can't be matched. Knowing that your hard work will pay off in the long run, you put in your best efforts to make your business a huge success.

When it comes to a job, you may work hard to meet monthly or yearly goals. However, it won't give you the sense of satisfaction that comes with owning a business.

Since you own the business, you are entitled to get credit for the success of your company. When your company makes profits and makes a difference in society, you would feel extremely happy and satisfied at your achievements.

5.3 Autonomy

Do you feel trapped in your current job and want to begin a career that gives you more freedom? Then the entrepreneurial world is waiting for you!

From time to time, you may hear the news that a CEOs or top manager left their high-paying corporate job to launch a startup. You may wonder why they decided to take this uneven path and gave up on the luxuries.

The answer is *freedom*!

When you work for someone else, you are answerable to the business owner. You can't follow your passion and may be forced to do tasks that are against your values.

On the other hand, you can feel free to take actions that are favorable for your future when you own a business. You can build your future by establishing a profitable business.

5.4   Never Get Bored

You work as an employee at a firm and find yourself checking time every now and then, waiting for the workday to end. You may feel bored with mundane tasks and plan to switch job for a more challenging role.

Does this scenario seem familiar? Then you should consider launching a startup to overcome boredom.

"Choose a job you love and you will never have to work a day in your life."

You won't find any entrepreneur complaining that their life is boring. Since they manage the entire firm, they find new challenges waiting for them on a daily basis. This provides them with the opportunity to learn new skills and stay engaged.

5.5   Become Independent

As per the economic report from April 2019, the unemployment rate in the US is 3.6%. You may believe that your job is safe and you can withdraw a handsome amount every month.

However, the situation isn't as favorable as you think. Economists believe that the US is likely to experience another major recession by the end of 2020. What if you lose your job because your company decides to downsize the workforce?

Instead of waiting for your boss to fire you, why don't you launch a startup and take your future in your own hands? This way, you can become financially independent and won't have to worry about losing your primary source of income.

When it comes to business, there is no limit. Through an effective strategy, you can earn a good income and secure your own future as well as that of your family.

5.6   Show Your Creativity

Not everyone can fit in the corporate culture. You may find yourself struggling at the job if you can't take orders from your superiors that are less smart than you.

Corporate environment tends to disregard the creativity of many smart people. If your boss doesn't appreciate you sharing your creative ideas, then it's time you should begin your entrepreneurial journey.

It's crucial for entrepreneurs to be creative. It's because they face various challenges and must come up with creative and innovative solutions to these problems.

Similarly, you need to launch new products and services to stay ahead of the competition and this is not possible without creative thinking.

When you own a business, you have the freedom to present creative ideas as well as implement them.

5.7   Create a Positive Work Culture

Organizational culture depicts moral values observed by a business and attitudes of the people working in that company. It is extremely important for building a strong relationship with customers as well as keeping the workforce engaged.

As per the Global Human Capital survey conducted in 2016, only 12% of top executives believe that the culture in their organization is just right.

By becoming an entrepreneur, you can take these matters in your hands and develop a culture that you find best. You can ensure that all the employees treat others well, maintain equality for all, observe moral values, and discourage behaviors and actions that can offend your employees, business partners or customers.

5.8   No Barriers to Growth

One of the major reasons why many people are turning to entrepreneurship and leaving their full-time jobs is because it gives them freedom and provides the chance to grow their professional career at a rapid pace.

Being a female professional, you may already have experienced some of the challenge's women face at the workplace. This includes pay gap, disregard of ideas presented by female employees, and glass ceiling which makes it extremely difficult for females to reach the management position in a firm.

However, if you don't want to worry about such issues anymore, then you should become an entrepreneur and work for your own goals.

Since you own the company, your professional growth is no more restricted by the corporate culture. You can grow your business globally and create a legacy that will be remembered for years to come.

5.9   Recognition

Shan-Lyn Ma, Neha Narkhede, Emily Leproust, and Jennifer Rubio – what is the similarity among these females?

They are successful US-based entrepreneurs who made their name through entrepreneurship. If they didn't follow their passion and stayed in a 9-to-5 job, no one would have known their name today.

This gives us the lesson that it's not easy to be recognized unless you take a leap and take action to make an impact in the world. An effective way to achieve this target is to start your own business.

As your business becomes successful, it will capture the attention of media and get people talking. While your workforce helps you manage business operations, the founder of the startup gets the most recognition. It's because a business can't be successful without the vision and efforts of the business owner.

5.10 Contribute to the Well-Being of Your Community

Your community is your identity. The people around you help you throughout your life. However, you may find it difficult to give back to society when you're working as a full-time employee due to financial problems and time constraints.

Entrepreneurship makes it easier for you to contribute to the well-being of others around you. When you launch a business, you create employment opportunities for them. You will feel satisfied upon helping others meet their needs.

Apart from financial assistance, you can also thank your community by dedicating time to help them out. For instance, if you notice any struggling entrepreneurs around you, you can arrange business training or life coaching sessions for them.

This way, not only can you help them build a better future, but also bring about a positive change in society.

"Remember that the happiest people are not those getting more, but those giving more."

- **H. Jackson Brown Jr.**

6. How to Launch Your Business Venture

It's a prevalent myth that you need to be well-educated to become a successful entrepreneur. However, many proclaimed entrepreneurs didn't graduate and still succeeded in making their name in the world.

For instance, Allison Statter, the confounder of Blended Strategy Group left the University of Arizona to pursue her passion, whereas Rachael Ray, a famous businesswoman and TV star, was also a college dropout.

All you need to begin the journey is a revolutionary business idea and the knowledge of basic business concepts and you're all set. Let's explore the business terminologies that you should know before launching your startup:

6.1 Business Plan

A business plan is the blueprint of your business that sets your direction. It depicts your goals as well as the path you will take to achieve those milestones.

Through a business plan, you can effectively pitch your startup idea to potential investors and convince them to fund your business. A thorough business plan makes it easier for you to make your place in the crowded market and manage business operations.

While a business plan should ideally span over 30-50 pages, you can also keep it short, so the stakeholders don't lose interest while reading it. The information you should include in the document includes:

6.1.1 Executive Summary
It provides a brief overview of the purpose of your business and should contain mission and vision statements.

6.1.2 Industry/Market Analysis
It explains the industry and market you intend to enter and highlights the sustainability factor of your business.

6.1.3 Competitive Analysis
In this section, you need to compare your startup with major competitors and pinpoint your competitive edge.

6.1.4 Product/Service
Add important information about your products and services to the document and explain how you will meet production challenges.

6.1.5 Financial Resources
This section should guide about the financial resources you would need to launch your business and keep it afloat.

6.1.6 Financial Projections
This includes information about the expected growth rate, revenue, and expenses for the upcoming 3-5 years.

6.1.7 Marketing/Sales Plan
Your business plan should clarify the marketing strategy to promote your brand.

6.1.8 SWOT Analysis

You must also emphasize on the strengths and weaknesses of your company as well as the opportunities and threats identified in the market through market research.

6.2 Business Credit

Also referred to as commercial credit, business credit score gives insights into the loan history of an organization. It explains whether or not the company is likely to return the loan amount based on the historical data.

Business credit is extremely important for small businesses. You may need funds to cover expenses and expand your business. Whether you apply for a loan with a bank or a private lender, they will check your credit history and score before approving your application.

If you have maintained a good credit score, you can get the required funds without having to rely on your personal credit score. Furthermore, this will increase your chances of qualifying for a loan at a low interest rate.

It's recommended to build a credit score since the day you launch your startup. Consequently, you won't have to worry about funds when an emergency arises. Here is how you can build business credit:

6.2.1   Set Up a Business Account

Open a bank account for your business at the earliest and use it to pay for business-related expenses. When you need a loan down the road, you can easily share account history with lenders.

6.2.2   Acquire Business Credit Cards

Using a credit card can benefit your business. It helps you improve your business credit score so you can qualify for a loan at low interest rates as and when needed.

6.2.3   Manage Credit Utilization

Acquiring a credit card isn't sufficient. You also need to utilize funds. However, make sure the ratio doesn't exceed 15% of the available credit if you don't want to hurt your credit score.

6.2.4   Never Delay Utility Bill Payments

You may delay the payment of utility bills, particularly when you need funds for other tasks. But doing so can negatively affect your business credit.

You should rather pay bills well in time and you will earn the reward in the form of a good credit score.

6.2.5   Maintain a Credit Line

You should use business credit cards to make payments to vendors and always clear payments in a timely manner. Make sure your suppliers report to the credit bureau so that every timely transaction is reflected on the credit report.

6.2.6   Remove Negative History

Credit history contains information about failure to return a loan, bankruptcies, liens, and judgments. This gives a negative impression and reduces your chances of qualifying for a loan.

However, if you talk to the agency and explain your situation, they may remove the record. This will help you keep your business credit clean.

6.2.7   Monitor Your Credit Score

Keep an eye on your business credit score and analyze from time to time how you can further improve the score. You can check your credit history via DUNS number.

6.3   Supply and Demand

The law of demand suggests that an increase in prices of goods, when other factors remain constant, leads to a decrease in the quantity demanded.

On the other hand, the law of supply states that if all other things remain constant, then a price increment results in an increase in quantity supplied.

However, the intensity with which quantity demanded and supplied are affected due to a price change may vary with elasticity. If your business deals in luxury goods, then a minor increase in price will significantly affect quantity. But the effect is completely opposite when it comes to staple goods for basic needs.

The concepts of supply and demand are extremely crucial because they help you choose the right pricing strategy for your business. Otherwise, you may set too high price and end up losing your customers or lose your profits due to low pricing.

6.4 Cash Flow

Cash flow provides detailed insights into the cash that moves in and out of a business during a specific time period. It is the representation of the firm's financial performance and the ability to stay in business.

Around 82% of small businesses launched every year fail due to cash flow problems. So, before you decide to become an entrepreneur, you should dig deeper into the basics of this important concept.

Businesses usually face the following cash flow problems:

- ➤ Bad debt
- ➤ Delayed payment of invoices by customers
- ➤ Short payment terms set by suppliers
- ➤ Low profit margins
- ➤ Ineffective inventory management

You need to address the aforementioned issues to improve cash flow and stabilize finances.

You should invest in inventory management software to bridge the gap. Many companies offer discounts to their customers upon early payment of dues. You can also revise policies to ensure that the payable time period balances receivable period.

The risk of bad debts can be decreased by conducting a credit check of new customers. Furthermore, you should consider increasing prices of your products and services.

6.5 Marketing Strategy

Marketing is the most crucial part of running a business. Unless your marketing campaigns effectively spread your brand message, how can you expect your target audience to notice you? However, keep in mind that your marketing efforts may go in vain if there's no strategy to support these campaigns.

A marketing strategy defines the direction for your marketing campaigns and ensures that they share consistent messages. While there's no hard and fast rule to design a strategy, you can make your marketing plans more impactful using the following steps:

- Define marketing budget
- Conduct market research to understand your audience
- State short-term and long-term business goals
- Evaluate marketing tactics of your competitors
- Note down your ideas and develop a strategy accordingly
- Test your strategy and make suitable changes as needed

In today's world, businesses can't survive in the competitive market for long if they don't maintain their online presence. You can set up a business website to reach global market. This gives your startup more exposure and builds credibility.

Once you finalize your business idea, you should establish your presence on social media platforms such as Facebook, Instagram, Snapchat, and LinkedIn. Not only are these platforms free, but they also allow you to build a community around your products and services.

Aside from free methods, you should also make the most of paid tools to capture the attention of potential customers. Unlike traditional marketing techniques, small businesses can reach their target audience through digital ads without breaking the bank.

For this purpose, you should develop an understanding of search ads, social media ads, and video ads. You can also opt for Pay-Per-Click ads that charge you a specific fee for every click on your ad instead of charging you for the duration during which the ad was displayed to the internet users.

7. Innovative Business Ideas for Women

Do you have any hobbies that keep you busy during spare time and refresh your mind? Why don't you turn this hobby into a business to earn money by doing what you like the most?

However, if you're not sure if it's a good idea to start a business based on your hobby, then don't worry. We have you covered!

Here are some small business ideas that you can adopt for your entrepreneurial venture:

7.1 Social Media Manager

Social media platforms make it easier for you to stay connected with your friends and family even if they are settled in the other corner of the world.

It's a prevalent misconception that social websites are only a waste of time. If you're aware of the benefits and the purposes of these digital platforms, you can make the most of them. In fact, you can begin your career as a social media marketer to bring your expertise to use.

A majority of businesses use social media to engage their customers and stay connected. You can launch your social media agency to help those businesses maintain their online presence.

Let's take a look at the most popular social platforms:

✓ Facebook and Facebook Messenger
✓ YouTube
✓ Instagram
✓ Twitter
✓ LinkedIn

7.2 Online Seller

Do you possess good negotiation and communication skills? Then it may be the right option for you to start selling goods online.

It's estimated that in 2019, around 1.92 billion people globally opt for shopping through e-commerce stores instead of visiting super stores physically. You can cash in on this opportunity and target this huge market.

You can utilize digital platforms to sell new goods or conduct garage sales online to earn a steady source of income.

7.3 Bike Rental Service

Cycling is a healthy hobby that improves your physical and mental health. Countries such as Netherlands promote this activity for the well-being of citizens and to control pollution which is a major concern around the globe.

With the increasing awareness about its benefits, people are turning to this healthy physical activity, but not everyone prefers buying a bicycle. You can offer a solution by providing bikes on rent.

You can also target tourists visiting the place, since they are interested in bike tours. Moreover, you can also arrange inline skates rentals for added benefits.

7.4 Fitness Center

Fitness conscious people are particular about gyms they visit and fitness trainers they work with. You can grab this opportunity and enter the $87.5 billion industry.

You would need exercise machines to launch this startup. However, make sure that the center is present at a central location where it is easily accessible to your target audience.

If you're a fitness trainer, then this business will work best for you. You can help people improve their physical health and build muscles. But if you don't have the certification, it's better to acquire the services of a professional trainer.

7.5 Food Business

Want to share your delicious cooking with others while generating income? You should consider entering the food industry due to its wide scope.

You would need sufficient financial resources and complete the legal procedure to launch a restaurant. On the other hand, starting a food truck business is relatively easier because it requires lesser resources and has a good chance of becoming successful in no time.

Apart from the driving license, you will need business license, EIN, food handling permit, health department permit, seller's permit, and other legal documents to become a businesswoman.

7.6   Graphic Designing

If you're creative and understand how to use digital tools, then a graphic designing business can be a good idea for you. You can offer your services to quality clients. Once the business grows, you can hire other professionals to help you out.

Service businesses are gaining popularity among entrepreneurs. However, you should cautiously define your mission and vision, objectives, and target market to become successful.

7.7   Personalized Gift Baskets

Back in the day, a majority of people preferred surprising their loved ones with handmade crafts. But in today's fast-paced world, people find it difficult to get time for such activities. You can launch a gift basket business and enable others to order personalized gift baskets for their loved ones.

Some companies choose special gifts for their employees on special occasions, but they don't have enough time to shop. You can reach out to such corporate customers and offer your services as a personal shopper.

7.8 Buy and Sell Website Domains

A website domain is the digital address of a website and acts as its identity. It's not difficult to buy and sell domains and therefore, you can easily launch a business by doing the same.

All you need to do is to buy high authority domains at reasonable rates and then you can resale them at a profit. However, you would need to conduct extensive online research to determine whether or not buying a particular domain would work in your favor.

7.9 Grocery Shopping

Everyone needs to buy groceries for their homes on a regular basis. While many online stores enable people to do shopping from the comfort of their homes, some people prefer to visit superstores physically since they either don't trust the quality of online goods or aren't much familiar with technology.

You can target such customers and offer to buy groceries. You can find many people interested in your services in your locality and can also use digital media to promote your business.

7.10 Home Cleaning and Clearance

Home cleaning business is one of the most in-demand startups and you can start it with minimal investment. All you need is cleaning equipment and appropriate licensing and you're all ready to earn good income. You can gain an edge over competitors by working on weekends as well.

Similarly, you can offer end of tenancy house cleaning and clearance services. Homeowners can acquire your services to clean the premises and get rid of junk.

7.11 Motivational Speaking

Some people are extremely good at communicating and possess the ability to motivate others through their thoughts. If you're one of them, you can start your career as a public speaker.

You can launch a YouTube channel to build an audience and contact event organizers to promote your personal brand. However, once your career progresses, you will get invitations without having to apply for speaking gigs.

7.12 Resume Writing Business

Regardless of which career a person chooses, they need an effective resume to get a job. You can launch a resume writing business to help job seekers make their resume more impactful.

The best thing about this business is that you can offer this service from your couch and find business via digital platforms.

Your business can design attractive resume and cover letter for job seekers and improve their chances of securing a good job. This way, not only can you generate income, but also achieve satisfaction that your efforts make an impact on society.

7.13 Event Planning

You are good at planning every detail of events and your friends consult you on special occasions such as weddings or birthday parties. Is that so? Then you'd be happy to know that you can become an entrepreneur by starting your event planning firm.

Creativity, time management, organizing, and communication are some of the most important skills when it comes to the event planning business.

7.14 Real Estate Agency

The importance of real estate business can never decrease despite the technological investments. You can start a real estate agency to help buyers and sellers with property dealings.

For this purpose, you ought to gain insights into the real estate industry. This way, you can assist your clients in making the right decisions. Furthermore, you should also learn about legal procedures to ensure your clients steer clear of legal issues.

7.15 Business Coaching

As your business flourishes, you will gain exposure and recognition. The growth provides you with the opportunity to explore new markets. You should think about offering business coaching and consultancy service to clients.

Aspiring entrepreneurs can benefit from your experiences and learn how to set up a business and run it successfully. Apart from offline training sessions, you can also design digital courses and sell them online to reach global audience.

8. Drawbacks of Entrepreneurship

Now that you know about the basics of running a startup, you may already have devised a plan to begin your entrepreneurial journey and make your dreams come true. But wait! There are a few things you should know before taking this route.

There are two sides to every coin. Despite the plethora of benefits that you can enjoy, there are certain negative aspects of entrepreneurship. Let's take a look at those and evaluate how you can use them to your advantage:

8.1   You Don't Get Off Days

Running a startup is not as easy as it seems. Unlike a job, there are no off days when it comes to entrepreneurship. You have to work for long hours to manage business activities.

However, working as an entrepreneur is extremely satisfying. You won't get tired knowing that your hard work today will benefit you in the long run.

8.2   Give Up Leisure

If you spend several hours every day, chatting with your friends or watching TV then be ready to give up spare time. When you become an entrepreneur, you don't get to enjoy free time as often. It won't be easy for you to indulge in your hobbies alongside running a business.

The positive side is that you will enjoy the hectic entrepreneurial life if you do what you love.

8.3 Burden of Responsibility

The burden of responsibility falls on your shoulders since you are the business owner. You have to work extremely hard to make your business a success. If there are huge losses, then you will suffer the most.

8.4 Financial Uncertainty

You should enter the world of entrepreneur only if you are a risk taker. The journey isn't easy as you lose job security and there is no guarantee that your business will generate profits.

But at the same time, you should keep in mind that entrepreneurship offers a myriad of benefits. If you are ready to bear the cons, then you can enjoy its advantages to the fullest.

8.5 Deal with Customers

Aside from increasing customer base, it's also the responsibility of an entrepreneur to achieve customer satisfaction. At times, it gets extremely difficult to satisfy the needs of your clients since you don't want to lose your valuable clients.

The key to resolving this issue is to offer quality products and services. You can also hire a customer support team to assist customers with their problems.

8.6 Risk Factors

Not all businesses are able to generate millions of dollars in revenue. Startups are risky ventures with a high risk of failure. As a result, you may end up losing your investment.

8.7 Increased Accountability

Running a business saves you from the hassles of working under a boss. But it also increases accountability. You are answerable to investors who have invested in your venture. You need to convince them about your sincerity before taking an important business decision.

8.8 Look for Funding

Startups often struggle with financial problems. As an entrepreneur, you ought to look for funding options and convince prospective investors to give your startup idea a try.

To achieve this goal, you need to believe in your idea and convince investors through supporting data.

8.9 Stress and Anxiety

Managing an entire business on your own can stress you out and cause anxiety. You have to be mentally strong and control your emotions. This will improve your mental health and help you become a better person on personal as well as professional level.

8.10   Keeping an Eye on Competitors

Regardless of how good your business idea, you can't sit idle even for a single idea. If you get lazy, it won't take long for your competitors to capture your customer base.

For this purpose, it's crucial for startups to stay active and keep working on innovative ideas. This will give you the chance to become a market leader as well as achieve the trust of your target audience.

Entrepreneurship has its own pros and cons. The purpose of sharing the disadvantages with you is to help you better understand this lesser-known world so you can come up with an effective strategy to become a successful entrepreneur.

Don't let the hardships break you. You should rather stay motivated and follow in the footsteps of well-known female entrepreneurs to reach where you want.

9. How to Become a Successful Entrepreneur

More than 627,000 new businesses are launched each year out of which 73% are owned by males while the rest are women-led. Despite the never-ending opportunities, a majority of these small businesses exit the market a short while later.

However, these statistics shouldn't instigate fear in you. If you follow the below-mentioned tips and guidelines, you will increase the chances of becoming a successful entrepreneur.

9.1 Develop Entrepreneurial Personality

Many entrepreneurs fail because they find it difficult to adopt an entrepreneurial mindset and personality. You should build mental strength to overcome setbacks and stay motivated.

Apart from being creative, you should also develop an optimistic mindset. As a result, you can focus on the holistic picture of the business and take your promising startup to new heights.

9.2 Learn, Learn, and Learn

The world around you is constantly changing and you can't succeed unless you keep learning new skills and adapt modern practices.

It's recommended to read motivational books and inspirational biographies of well-known entrepreneurs. You can also stay up-to-date with technological and business advancements through blogs and e-magazines.

9.3 Aim for Long-Term Achievements

When it comes to a business, you need to set long-term goals and then divide them into short-term objectives.

Make sure your goals aren't ambiguous to achieve the desired results.

For instance, instead of saying that you want to increase sales, you should set a more specific goal. Here are some examples for your guidance:

- To increase monthly sales by 20% over the next quarter
- To reduce employee turnover rate by 10% during the next 2 months
- To increase traffic to the business website by 10% during the next 3 months while reducing digital marketing costs by 5%

Such goals keep you focused towards goal attainment and you can monitor performance more effectively.

9.4   Don't Take Everything Personal

You should see the world differently from others so as to stand out from the crowd. Your unique approach will attract criticism as well, but make sure you don't take everything personally.

Constructive criticism can help you improve business practices. However, if you believe that people criticizing your business actually hold a personal grudge against you, then you are missing the point.

As an entrepreneur, you should learn to be professional. Be ready to listen to others and use this information to make your business successful.

9.5   Manage Time

Time management is the most important character tactic of successful entrepreneurs. They make the most of their time to carry out business-related tasks as well as manage their personal life.

Steve Jobs, the founder and CEO of Apple, Pixar, and NeXT is known for his remarkable business achievements. But when he died, he regretted always ignoring his family and personal life.

Entrepreneurship brings along the feeling of achievement and satisfaction, but if you don't manage your time and fail to spend your time with family or ignore your hobbies, then you will end up regretting the decision of launching a startup.

You don't want that, right?

9.6   Build a Trustworthy Team

Not many people feel comfortable with the idea of delegating tasks and prefer working alone. However, the key to building a profitable business is to learn the skill of teamwork.

As a business owner, you are responsible to ensure that business operations run smoothly. If you try to do everything on your own, your business will suffer.

You ought to build a trustworthy team by onboarding talented staff. If you provide a great working environment, offer monetary and non-monetary benefits, and value your employees, they will work their best to achieve company goals.

9.7 Align Your Marketing Strategy

Businesses spend 7-8% of their annual gross revenue on marketing activities. It's extremely important to promote your brand through different mediums. Unless your target audience is aware of your product and services, how can you expect them to support your business?

However, many small businesses end up wasting their market budget. It's because they fail to understand which marketing methods and strategies would work best for them.

Before you launch a marketing campaign, make sure you have a complete strategy and marketing plan in hand. Be consistent with your marketing efforts and deliver a message that resonates with your existing and potential customers. This will effectively reduce marketing expenses.

9.8 Monitor Finances

A good entrepreneur understands business financials and monitors revenue, expenses, assets, and liabilities. If you don't keep an eye on finances, you may end up wasting resources.

It's not necessary to get a degree in business administration to become an entrepreneur. You can enroll in free online courses to get a basic understanding of business finances. This will definitely help you in the long run.

9.9 Improve Communication Skills

While your team will help you with business operations, you have to represent your company at different forums. Aside from pitching the idea to investors, you may also have to attend public speaking events to spread the word about your startup.

You should overcome your fear and improve your communication skills. Your network can help you in this regard. Moreover, you can also learn from your mentor or watch videos of successful entrepreneurs to learn from them.

9.10 Risk Management

Startups involve various risks and the inability to reduce those risks leads to business failure. During the initial stage, you must identify potential risks and develop a strategy to tackle them in a hassle-free manner.

Unforeseen circumstances can ruin your entrepreneurial efforts. But if you predict the future and come up with plans A and B, you will find it easier to handle risk and emerge successful in every situation.

9.11 Focus On Your Target Audience

A business becomes successful when it addresses a particular problem and fulfills the expectations of the target audience. Any new idea must be evaluated to ensure that it adds value to customers and is likely to be appreciated.

For this purpose, you should conduct comprehensive market surveys and learn about the preferences of your valuable customer base.

9.12 Never Ignore Customer Feedback

Customer feedback gives you the opportunity to improve your business. Whenever any customer shares a review of your product or service, you should pay attention and take actions to improve their experience with your brand.

Apart from asking for customer feedback, you should also share your business processes and strategies with mentors. They can guide you about the best practices and help you grow personally and professionally.

If you are active on social media, you can ask your followers to leave a review on your business page. This way, you can answer their concerns, engage followers, and establish goodwill.

10. Conclusion

Entrepreneurs are the major asset of a nation that support the economy of the country and play a crucial role in the development of society. Not only do they create employment opportunities, but also positively influence others through their achievements.

While many people are afraid to act on their dreams, you should launch your startup to become a person you always aspired to be. Don't pay heed to those who discourage you from taking this leap and get ready to achieve success.

You can launch a business depending on the available financial resources. For instance, you can offer lawn services or sell your paintings if you're good at it. This means you can convert your hobby into a business and earn income for a living.

The entrepreneurial journey isn't as easy as many people wrongly believe. You are likely to come across failure, stress, financial issues, and many other problems along the way. But the good thing is that the pros of entrepreneurship outweigh its cons.

When you begin your entrepreneurial journey, you get the chance to improve your financial conditions and become independent. This way, you can achieve self-satisfaction and work hard to make your dreams come true.

Entrepreneurship offers freedom from a job and enables you to work for your dreams. You can show your creativity to make your business a success and learn quite a lot about different aspects of running a business through your own experiences.

While you enjoy the perks of entrepreneurship, don't forget your community and people around you who helped you achieve your goals.

You will find many struggling people who need motivation to change their lives. You should always be ready to give back to society and help such individuals.

It's not always necessary to support them financially. You can motivate them through your uplifting thoughts. It is also a good idea to arrange business coaching sessions for aspiring female entrepreneurs and support them in establishing their venture.

Female entrepreneurs are the backbone of society and the number of female-owned businesses is on a rise. They tend to become successful mainly because of their strong character traits such as resilience, emotional strength, persistence, multitasking, and organization.

So, it's time you should become an entrepreneur and launch a business that will make your proud.

Angela K. Chambers

Go Ahead Start
Your JOURNEY to SUCCESS!

11. Bibliography

2019 Small Business Trends. (2019). Retrieved from Guidant Financial: https://www.guidantfinancial.com/small-business-trends/

Alton, L. (2018, December 28). *Fascinating Pros and Cons to an Online Business You MUST Know for Success.* Retrieved from Small Business Trends: https://smallbiztrends.com/2018/07/ecommerce-advantages-and-disadvantages.html

Carbajo, M. (2017, March 10). *10 Stats That Explain Why Business Credit is Important for Small Business.* Retrieved from SBA: https://www.sba.gov/blog/10-stats-explain-why-business-credit-important-small-business

Crowdfunding. (n.d.). Retrieved June 26, 2019, from Investopedia: https://www.investopedia.com/terms/c/crowdfunding.asp

Fitness Industry Statistics. (2017, December 13). Retrieved from Welness Creative Co.: https://www.wellnesscreatives.com/fitness-industry-statistics-growth/

Gale, T. (2008). *Introduction: Entrepreneurship.* Retrieved from Encyclopedia.com: https://www.encyclopedia.com/finance/encycl

opedias-almanacs-transcripts-and-
maps/introduction-entrepreneurship

Hull, P. (2013, June 21). *Joint Ventures Provide
Opportunities for Entrepreneurs*. Retrieved from
Forbes:
https://www.forbes.com/sites/patrickhull/2013
/06/21/joint-ventures-provide-opportunities-
for-entrepreneurs

MacNeil, N. (n.d.). *10 Challenges Women Entrepreneurs
Are Facing and What WE Are Doing About It*.
Retrieved from She Takes On the World:
https://shetakesontheworld.com/thousand-
women-wrong/

Matt. (2013, October 25). *How "Dreaming Big" Helps
You As An Entrepreneur*. Retrieved from
Under30CEO:
https://under30ceo.com/dreaming-big-helps-
entrepreneur/

Previte, J. (2019, February 11). *The 2019 Digest of the
Most Valuable Company Culture Statistics*.
Retrieved from BlueLeadz:
https://www2.deloitte.com/insights/us/en/focu
s/human-capital-trends/2016/human-capital-
trends-introduction.html

The top 10 traits of successful, creative businesswomen.
        (2012, March 8). Retrieved from The Guardian:
        https://www.theguardian.com/culture-
        professionals-network/culture-professionals-
        blog/2012/mar/08/successful-businesswomen-
        top-ten-traits